# Earthquake Safety Guide for Homeowners

FEMA 530 / September 2005

## Publishing Information

*The Homeowner's Guide to Earthquake Safety* was originally developed and published by the California Seismic Safety Commission. This modified version of the Guide was developed by FEMA in cooperation with the California Seismic Safety Commission staff. The original guide was prepared for publication by the staff of the Collaborative for Disaster Mitigation, San Jose State University.

## Ordering Information

Copies of this publication are available from the FEMA Distribution Facility. To order, call 1-800-480-2520 and ask for FEMA publication 530.

## On the cover:

Taken in Atascadero, California, on January 25, 2004, the photograph shows a home that slid 2 feet off its foundation as a result of the 6.5 San Simeon Earthquake.

# CONTENTS

California Homeowners: This Guide does **not** cover real estate disclosure requirements and related recommendations as described in the California Seismic Safety Commission publication *The Homeowner's Guide to Earthquake Safety*. To obtain that guide, go to http://www.seismic.ca.gov/sscpub.htm.

# ACKNOWLEDGMENTS

## Department of Homeland Security, Federal Emergency Management Agency

Elizabeth Lemersal

Jeffrey Lusk

## Seismic Safety Commission

Lucille M. Jones, Ph.D., Chair, *Seismology*

Hon. Richard Alarcon, *State Senate*
(Chris Modrzejewski)

Hon. Carol Liu, *State Assembly*
(Donald Manning)

Lawrence T. Klein, *Utilities*

Mark Church, *Local Government*

Linden Nishinaga, P.E., *City Government*

Celestine Palmer, *Insurance*

Andrew A. Adelman, P.E., *Cities/Building Official*

Stan Moy, A.I.A., *Architecture and Planning*

Daniel Shapiro, S.E., *Structural Engineering*

Vacant, *Mechanical Engineering*

Bruce R. Clark, Ph.D., *Geology*

Vacant, *County Government*

Vacant, *Emergency Services*

Donald R. Parker, Vice Chairman, *Fire Protection*

Jimmie R. Yee, *Social Services*

Vacant, *Soils Engineering*

## Seismic Safety Commission Staff

Richard McCarthy, Executive Director

Robert Anderson

Karen Cogan

Henry Reyes

Henry Sepulveda

Fred Turner, Project Coordinator

Sue Celli

Rebecca Romo

## Collaborative for Disaster Mitigation Staff

Guna Selvaduray, Ph.D., Executive Director

Patrick Chong, Webmaster

Crystal Carrera, Administrative Assistant

## The Commission gratefully acknowledges the assistance of the following:

American Red Cross

American Society of Home Inspectors

Association of Bay Area Governments

Building Education Center

California Association of Realtors

California Building Officials

California Council of the American Institute of Architects

California Geological Survey

California Real Estate Inspection Association

California Governor's Office of Emergency Services

City of Los Angeles

Earthquake Engineering Research Institute

Humboldt Earthquake Education Center

International Code Council

SBC

San Diego Association of Governments

Southern California Association of Governments

Southern California Association of Residential Retrofit Professions

Southern California Gas Company/Sempra

Structural Engineers Association of California

Committee on Earthquake Safety Issues for Gas Systems

# INTRODUCTION

**Earthquakes**, especially major ones, are dangerous, inevitable, and a fact of life in some parts of the United States. Sooner or later another "big one" will occur.

Earthquakes:

- Occur without warning
- Can be deadly and extremely destructive
- Can occur at any time

As a current or potential owner of a home*, you should be very concerned about the potential danger to not only yourselves and your loved ones, but also to your property.

The major threats posed by earthquakes are bodily injuries and property damage, which can be considerable and even catastrophic.

Most of the property damage caused by earthquakes ends up being handled and paid for by the homeowner.

- In a 2000 study titled *HAZUS 99: Average Annual Earthquake Losses for the United States*, FEMA estimated U.S. losses from earthquakes at $4.4 billion per year.

- Large earthquakes in or near major urban centers will disrupt the local economy and can disrupt the economy of an entire state.

However, proper earthquake preparation of your home can:

- Save lives
- Reduce injuries
- Reduce property damage

*For the purpose of this document, "home" includes single-family residences, duplexes, triplexes, and fourplexes.

As a homeowner, you can **significantly reduce** damage to your home by fixing a number of known and common weaknesses.

This booklet is a good start to begin strengthening your home against earthquake damage.

It describes:

- Common weaknesses that can result in your home being damaged by earthquakes, and

- Steps you can take to correct these weaknesses.

*There are no guarantees of safety during earthquakes, but properly constructed and strengthened homes are far less likely to collapse or be damaged during earthquakes. FEMA advises you to act on the suggestions outlined in this booklet and make yourself, your family, and your home safer.*

# EXAMPLES OF DAMAGE TO SINGLE-FAMILY HOMES

Figure 1 - San Fernando Earthquake, Feb. 9, 1971 Severely damaged split level one- and two-story wood frame dwelling. The one-story portion dropped about 3 feet.

Figure 2 - Loma Prieta Earthquake, Oct. 17, 1989 Home moved off of its foundation and was considered a total loss.

Figure 3 - Northridge Earthquake, Jan. 17, 1994 Single-family residence damaged due to failure of multiple elements.

Figure 4 - Northridge Earthquake, Jan. 17, 1994 Chimney collapse - common type of damage to unreinforced masonry.

Figure 5 - San Simeon Earthquake, Dec. 22, 2003 This home slid 2 feet off its foundation due to inadequate nailing of walls to its sill plates.

Figure 6 - San Simeon Earthquake, Dec. 22, 2003 The collapsed porch was not adequately attached to this single-family residence.

# EARTHQUAKE HAZARDS IN THE UNITED STATES

Earthquakes strike suddenly, without warning. Earthquakes can occur any time of the year and at any time of the day or night. On a yearly basis, 70 to 75 damaging earthquakes occur throughout the world. Estimates of losses from a future earthquake in the United States approach $200 billion. Forty-five states and territories in the United States are at moderate to very high risk from earthquakes, and they are located in every region of the country.

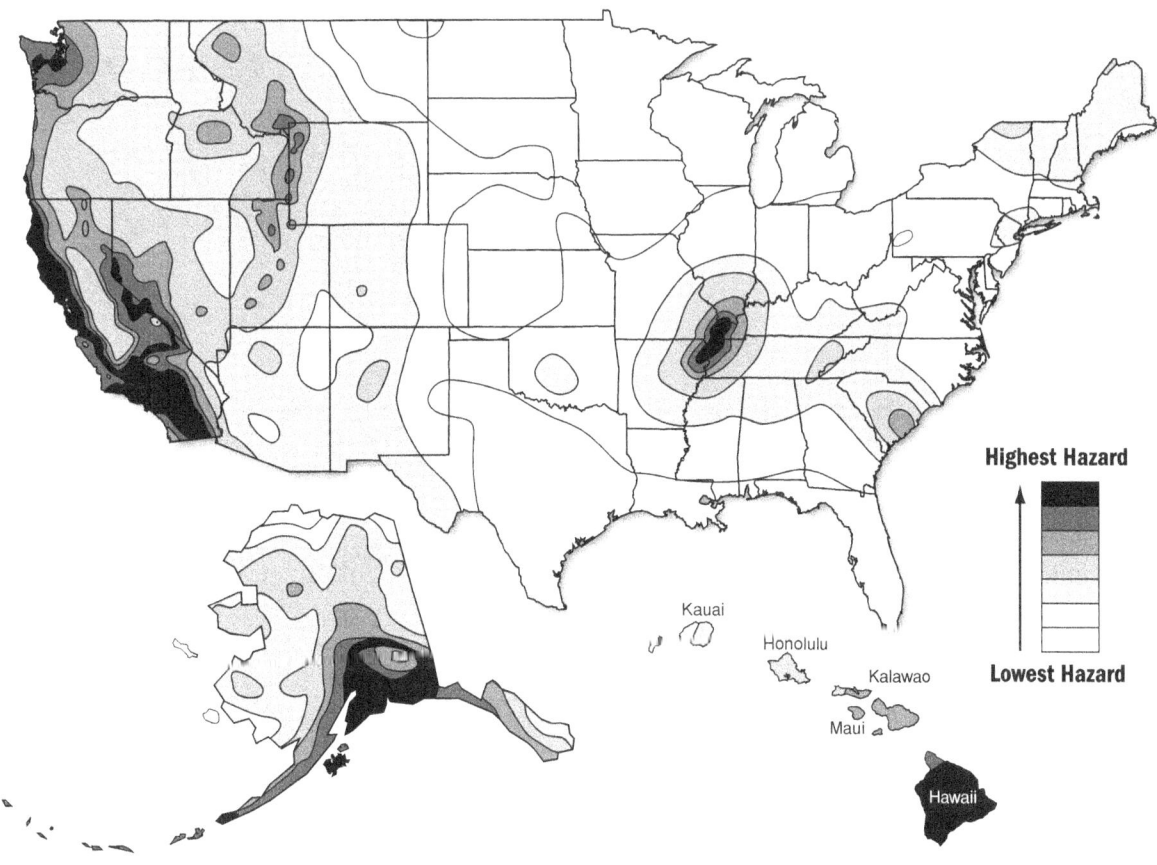

Earthquake hazards in the United States. This map is based on seismicity and fault-slip rates and takes into account the frequency of occurrence of earthquakes of various magnitudes. Locally, the hazard may be greater than that shown, because site geology may amplify ground motions. Based on U.S. Geological Survey National Seismic Hazard Map for the Coterminous United States (http:// eqhazmaps.usgs.gov/html/map_graphic.html).

# EARTHQUAKE WEAKNESSES

The earthquake weaknesses identified in this section, if not corrected, can result in one or more of the following:

- Injury to occupants
- Severe damage to your home
- Broken gas and utility lines
- Fires from broken gas lines
- Damage to floors, walls, and windows
- Damage to the contents in the house
- Damage to the foundations

*Please remember that:*

- Retrofitting before an earthquake is relatively cheap.
- Doing major structural repairs to your home after an earthquake is very expensive.
- Sometimes the damage is extensive enough to require the entire house to be demolished.
- After an earthquake, there is usually a shortage of available licensed contractors and engineers in the impacted area, because of the sudden high demand for their services.
- An appropriate seismic retrofit will reduce damage and save you money.

*Please consult your local Building Department and/or a licensed architect or engineer for more detailed information.*

# Unbraced Water Heaters

## The Problem

If water heaters are not properly braced, they can topple over during an earthquake, causing:

- Broken gas lines and gas leaks
- Fires resulting in major damage to homes
- Broken water lines and flooding

## How to Identify

✓ Is the water heater freestanding?

✓ Are there straps or other types of restraints securing the water heater?

✓ Are there straps or restraints bolted to the studs?

✓ Are there flexible pipes for water and gas connected to the water heater?

## Remember

- Replacing a water heater after an earthquake can cost more than $500.
- Repairing fire damage and flooding damage can cost several thousand dollars, including the entire cost of your home!
- There are many different ways of strapping a water heater. One example is shown on the next page.
- Check with your local Building Department for details of local requirements.
- Know where your main water valve is so that you can shut it off if you have a water leak.
- Know where your main gas valve is so that you can shut it off if you hear or smell a gas leak. *(See page 25)*

Water heater

**Figure 7** - The unbraced water heater in this home fell during an earthquake; the resulting fire destroyed the home.

**Figure 8** - This unstrapped water heater tipped over during the 1984 Morgan Hill Earthquake. Fortunately, gas and water lines were not ruptured.

# Brace Water Heaters

*Water heaters must be braced (securely attached) to the studs in a wall.*

## The Solution

There are many solutions – all relatively inexpensive.

- Purchase and install a strap kit or bracing kit from your local hardware store.

Other options include:

- Have a licensed plumber strap your water heater according to code.

- Use metal tubing or heavy metal strapping and lag screws and washers to secure the water heater to the wall studs.

The gas and water lines should also have flexible pipes. These are safer than rigid pipes during an earthquake.

Be sure to check the straps once a year. They may come loose due to vibrations, or other causes.

## How-to Resources

- Your local home improvement store

- Go to www.fema.gov, and under the Earthquake section, search for "Brace Hot Water Heaters" for specific bracing instructions.

- Publication: Guidelines for Earthquake Bracing of Residential Water Heaters. Department of General Services, Division of the State Architect, revised August 11, 2004. Available online at http://www.documents.dgs.ca.gov/dsa/pubs/ waterheaterbracing_08-11-04.pdf.

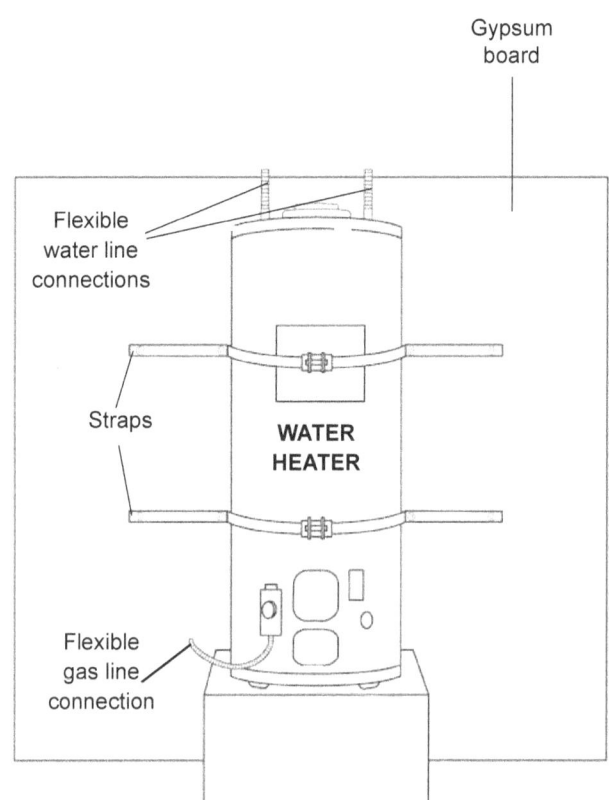

Gypsum board

Flexible water line connections

Straps

WATER HEATER

Flexible gas line connection

**Figure 9 - One method of water heater bracing.** Straps and screws visible with water heater in a garage installation.

| Comparison of Cost:  Preventing vs. Repairing Earthquake Damage | |
| --- | --- |
| **Project Cost** | **Cost to Repair After an Earthquake** |
| $20 to $200 | $500 to total value of home (if completely destroyed) |

# Home Not Anchored to Foundation

## The Problem

Houses that are not bolted to the foundation can move off their foundations during earthquakes.

## How to Identify

- ✓ Go down into the crawl space – the area between the first floor and the foundation – to find out if your house is bolted to its foundation.

- ✓ Look for the heads of anchor bolts that fasten the sill plate – the wooden board that sits directly on top of the foundation – securely to the foundation. *(See Figure 11a, page 8)*

- ✓ You should be able to see the large nuts, washers, and anchor bolts, installed at least every 4 to 6 feet along the sill plate. Steel plates are sometimes used instead of anchor bolts. *(See Figure 11b, page 8)*

## Remember

- It is very expensive to lift a house, and place it back on its foundation.

- Homes moving off their foundations can cause gas lines to rupture, which in turn can result in fires.

*Office of Emergency Services*

**Figure 10** - This home wasn't bolted and slid off its foundation. Sometimes the damage can be so bad that houses have to be demolished.

*If your home has no foundation, or an old concrete foundation, see page 23.*

## Slab Foundations

Some homes are built directly on concrete slabs. These houses do not have crawl spaces and foundation walls.

Nearly all homes with slab foundations that were originally built to code will have anchor bolts or straps.

However, if the house is not bolted to the slab, you have an earthquake weakness.

Newer homes generally have anchor bolts or straps.

If you have an unfinished garage, you may be able to see the anchor bolts.

You are not required to remove siding, drywall, or plaster to determine if your house has anchor bolts.

# Anchor Foundation

## The Solution

Drill holes through the sill plate into the foundation and install anchor bolts. *(See Figure 11a)*

If there is not enough room to drill, you can attach steel plates to hold the sill plate to the foundation. *(See Figure 11b)*

Anchor bolts have to be installed properly for them to be effective.

You must obtain the proper permits from your local Building Department before beginning work.

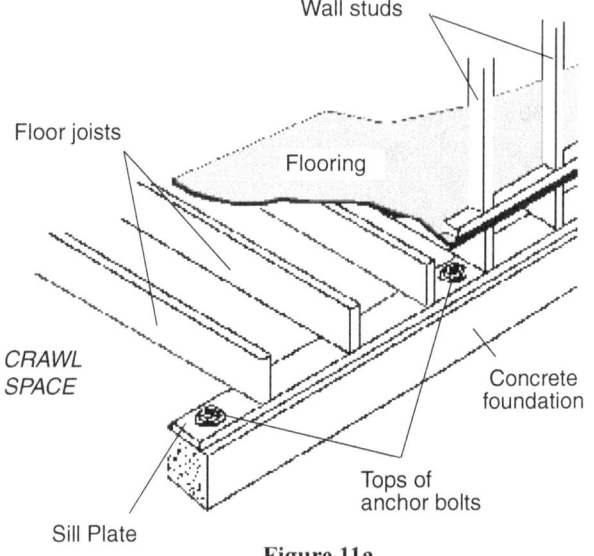

**Figure 11a**

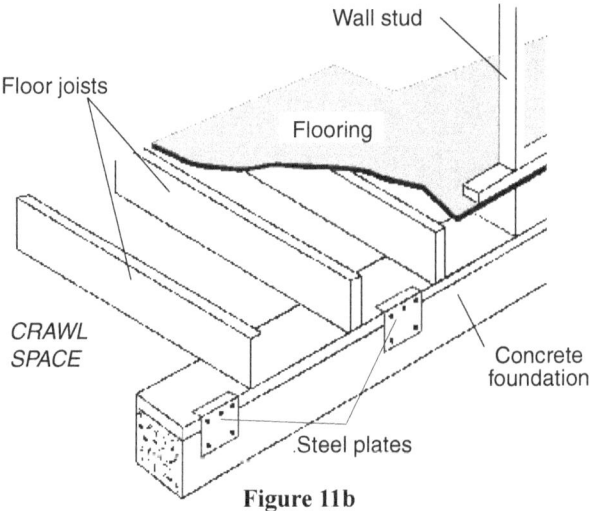

**Figure 11b**

## How-to Resources

- Detailed information for do-it-yourselfers or engineers can be found in the <u>International Existing Building Code</u>, published by the International Code Council.

- Go to www.fema.gov, and under the Earthquake section, search for "Strengthen Foundation Walls" for specific anchoring instructions.

**Figure 11 - Anchor bolts or steel plates.** A home's crawl space may be formed by a wood stud wall *(see next page for description)* between the foundation and the floor joists or the floor joists may rest directly on the sill plate. In either case, you should be able to see the heads of anchor bolts or steel plates installed at appropriate intervals. These fixtures fasten the sill plate to the foundation.

| Comparison of Cost:  Preventing vs. Repairing Earthquake Damage | |
| --- | --- |
| **Project Cost** | **Cost to Repair After an Earthquake** |
| $250 to $5,000 | $25,000 to total value of home (if completely destroyed) |

# Weak Crawl Space Walls

## The Problem

Wooden floors and stud walls are sometimes built on top of an exterior foundation to support a house and create a crawl space. *(See Figure 14, page 10)*

These stud walls carry the weight of the house.

During an earthquake, these walls can collapse if they are not braced to resist horizontal movement.

If the wall fails, the house may shift or fall.

## How to Identify

✓ Go under the house through the crawl space, to see if there are any wood stud walls.

✓ If there are such walls, check to see if they are braced.

✓ There should be plywood panels adequately nailed to the studs OR there should be diagonal wood sheathing. *(See Figure 13)*

✓ If you have neither of these, the walls are probably insufficiently braced or unbraced.

✓ Horizontal or vertical wood siding is not strong enough to brace these walls.

## Remember

■ It is very expensive to lift a house, repair these walls, and put it back on its foundation.

*Office of Emergency Services*

**Figure 12** - Damage to home due to crawl space wall failure.

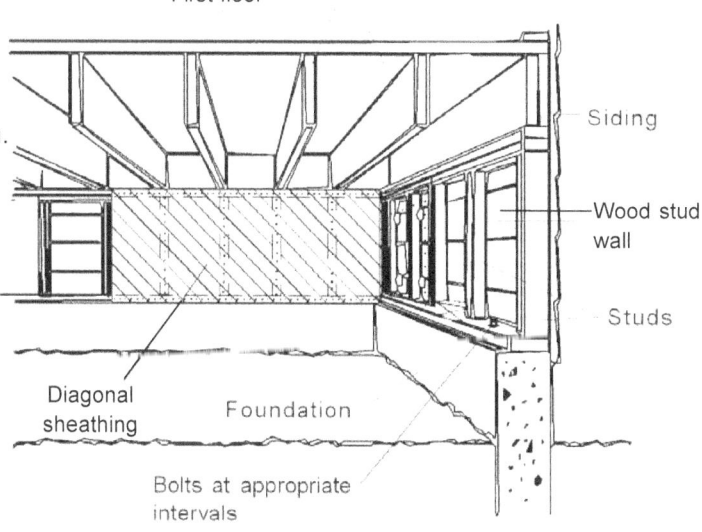

Floor joists

First floor

Siding

Wood stud wall

Studs

Diagonal sheathing

Foundation

Bolts at appropriate intervals

**Figure 13 - Diagonal sheathing.** Common in older homes.

## The Solution

Plywood, or other wood products allowed by code, should be nailed to the studs.

The following are important:

- Type of wood product used
- Plywood thickness
- Nail size and spacing
- Not covering vents

Consult your local Building Department for permit requirements before starting work.

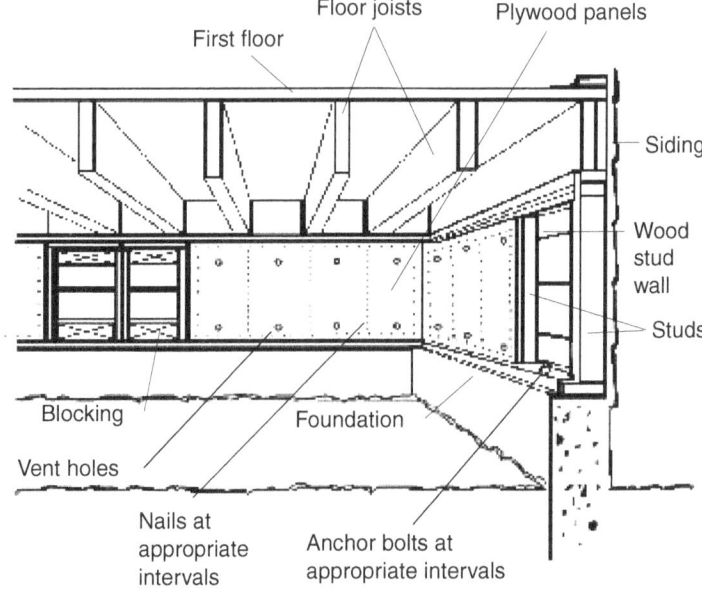

First floor — Floor joists — Plywood panels — Siding — Wood stud wall — Studs — Blocking — Foundation — Vent holes — Nails at appropriate intervals — Anchor bolts at appropriate intervals

**Figure 14 - Plywood or diagonal sheathing strengthens weak wood stud walls.** If your home has a wood stud wall between the foundation and the first floor, and the wall is not braced with plywood or diagonal sheathing, the house may fall or shift off its foundation during an earthquake.

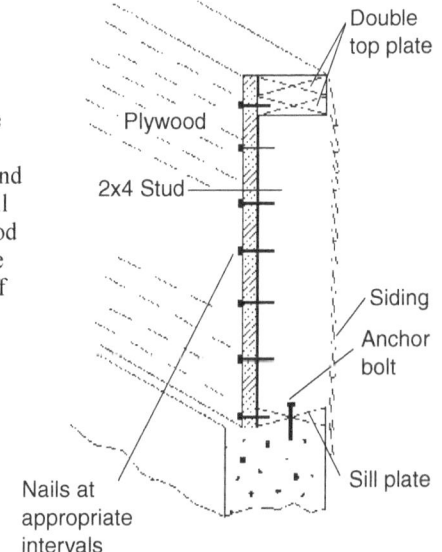

Double top plate — Plywood — 2x4 Stud — Siding — Anchor bolt — Sill plate — Nails at appropriate intervals

## How-to Resources

- Detailed information for do-it-yourselfers or engineers can be found in the International Existing Building Code, published by the International Code Council

- Go to www.fema.gov, and under the Earthquake section, search for "Strengthen Foundation Walls" for specific strengthening instructions.

**Comparison of Cost:  Preventing vs. Repairing Earthquake Damage**

| Project Cost | Cost to Repair After an Earthquake |
|---|---|
| $500 to $2,500 | $25,000 to total value of home (if completely destroyed) |

# Pier-and-Post Foundations

## The Problem

The outside of the house is supported by wood posts resting on unconnected concrete piers. Siding is often nailed to the outside of the posts, making them not easily visible.

During an earthquake these posts can fail, if they are not braced against swaying.

If the posts fail, the house may shift or fall.

## How to Identify

- ✓ Go under the house to see if there is a continuous foundation under the outside walls.

- ✓ If you do not see a continuous foundation, you may have an earthquake weakness.

- ✓ If you see only unconnected concrete piers and wood posts, or only wood posts, supporting the outside walls, you have an earthquake weakness.

## Remember

- ■ Horizontal or vertical wood siding is not strong enough to brace pier-and-post foundations.

- ■ Major structural repairs, like lifting an entire house to repair the posts and putting it back, are very expensive.

**Figure 15** - The pier-and-post foundation under this home shifted during a recent earthquake.

## The Solution

Consult a licensed architect or engineer, and a licensed building contractor who specializes in foundations, to fix this problem.

It may be possible to make the foundation safer by bracing the posts.

You might be better off to add a new foundation and plywood walls in the crawl space to make sure that the house will not shift or fall off its foundation during an earthquake.

## How-to Resource

- Detailed information for engineers can be found in the International Existing Building Code, published by the International Code Council.

### Comparison of Cost: Preventing vs. Repairing Earthquake Damage

| Project Cost | Cost to Repair After an Earthquake |
|---|---|
| $1,000 to $25,000 | $20,000 to total value of home (if completely destroyed) |

# Unreinforced Masonry Foundations

## The Problem

Unreinforced masonry—brick, concrete block, or stone—foundations often cannot resist earthquake shaking. They may break apart, or be too weak to hold anchor bolts. Homes may shift off such foundations during earthquakes, damaging the walls, floors, utility lines, and home contents.

## How to Identify

✓ If your home's foundation is brick or stone, and looks like one of the foundations shown in the photos here, it is probably unreinforced.

✓ If there is a space filled with grout between the inner and outer faces of a brick foundation (where anchor bolts and reinforcing steel could be installed), it may be reinforced.

✓ If the outside of the foundation is covered, you may have to look under the house to see the type of foundation you have.

✓ If you are not sure what to look for, seek the services of a licensed engineer to determine if your foundation is reinforced or not.

## Remember

■ It is cheaper to do this before an earthquake damages the house than after.

Figure 16 - This is an unreinforced stone foundation. They typically fail during earthquakes.

Figure 17 - Note the bricks exposed in this unreinforced masonry foundation.

## The Solution

There are several ways to fix this problem.

The most common approach is to replace all or part of the existing foundation with a poured reinforced concrete foundation.

Another solution is strengthening the unreinforced brick or stone foundation, which is generally expensive.

Seek the help of a licensed architect or engineer, and a licensed foundation contractor or general contractor.

## How-to Resource

- Detailed information for engineers can be found in the International Existing Building Code, published by the International Code Council.

| Comparison of Cost:  Preventing vs. Repairing Earthquake Damage | |
| --- | --- |
| **Project Cost** | **Cost to Repair After an Earthquake** |
| $15,000 to $50,000 | $15,000 to total value of home (if completely destroyed) |

# Homes Built on Steep Hillsides

## The Problem

Houses built on the sides of steep hills are often set on exposed posts or columns, as shown in the Figures 18 and 19.

The potentially hazardous conditions that are unique to homes on steep hillsides are:

- Stilt-type posts with or without diagonal bracing

- Walls with very different heights or that are stepped or sloped down the hillsides.

If these posts or walls are not properly braced, they may collapse during an earthquake.

Sometimes, the supports on the downhill side will be hidden behind a tall wall that encloses a large unfinished space. (This is similar to, but taller than, a crawl space under a typical house built on flat ground.)

## How to Identify

✓ Is the house located on a slope?

✓ Are the columns or walls supporting the home braced?

✓ If you are not sure if there is bracing or if the bracing is adequate, consult a licensed engineer.

## Remember

- It is very expensive to lift a house, repair the posts, and put it back.

*Office of Emergency Services*

**Figure 18** - This hillside home was built on an unbraced tall wall that failed.

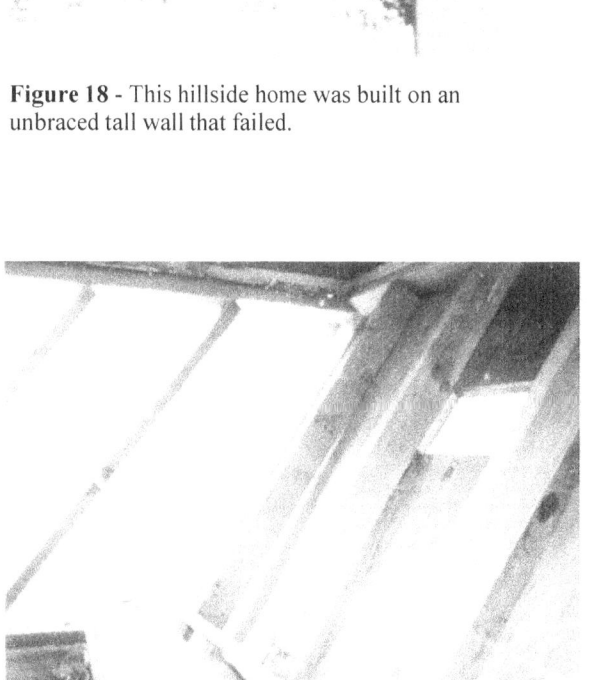

*Office of Emergency Services*

**Figure 19** - This photograph shows an interior detail of a home similar to the one above, with substantial damage to a building with an unbraced tall wall.

## The Solution

Consult a licensed architect or engineer, and a licensed contractor, to fix this problem.

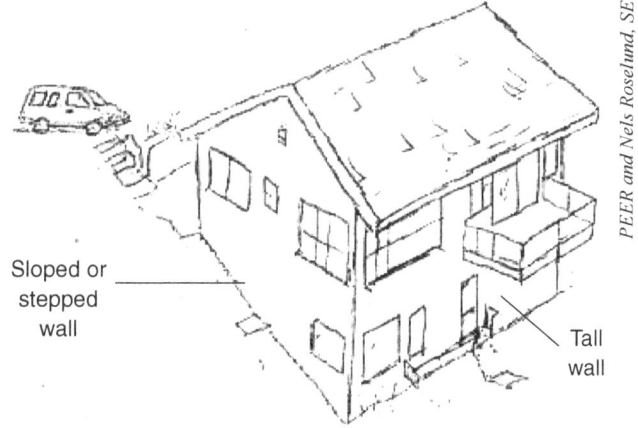

*PEER and Nels Roselund, SE*

Sloped or stepped wall

Tall wall

**Figure 20** - Hillside homes with sloped and tall walls or posts require special engineering.

## How-to Resources

- Detailed information can be found in the International Existing Building Code, published by the International Code Council.

| Comparison of Cost: Preventing vs. Repairing Earthquake Damage | |
| --- | --- |
| **Project Cost** | **Cost to Repair After an Earthquake** |
| $1,000 to $50,000 | $10,000 to total value of home (if completely destroyed) |

# Unreinforced Masonry Walls

## The Problem

Houses built of unreinforced masonry – bricks, hollow clay tiles, stone, concrete blocks, or adobe – are very likely to be damaged during earthquakes.

The mortar holding the masonry together is generally not strong enough to resist earthquake forces.

Anchorage of walls to the floor and the roof is critical.

These houses are weak (brittle) and can break apart.

Walls may fall away or buckle, resulting in damage.

**Figure 21** - The plaster-covered brick walls of this building collapsed during a recent earthquake.

## How to Identify

✓ Can bricks or stone be seen from the outside (unless the walls are covered with stucco)?

✓ Do the brick walls have "header courses" of bricks turned endways every five or six rows? *(See Figure 22)*

✓ Was the house built before 1940?

If you cannot tell from the outside, turn off the power and take the cover plate off one of the electrical outlet boxes on an outside wall and look for brick or other masonry.

If the wall is concrete or concrete block, it is very difficult to find out if reinforcing steel was added during construction.

You will then need:

■ The house's plans, which may be on file with the Building Department, or

■ To consult a licensed engineer to make the determination.

**Figure 22** - Header courses of bricks are usually placed endwise every six or so rows in unreinforced masonry walls to tie the outer layer of bricks to the layers inside the wall.

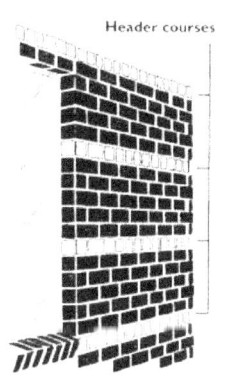

## Remember

■ It is very expensive to shore up a house, remove damaged walls, and put in new walls.

## The Solution

Consult a licensed architect or engineer to fix this problem.

One solution may involve:

- Tying the walls to the floor and roof
- Installing a steel frame and bolting the wall to it.

*Jessica Tran*

**Figure 23** - Unreinforced masonry wall strengthened by installing a steel frame inside.

*Jessica Tran*

**Figure 24** - Bolting of unreinforced masonry wall to steel frame on the inside.

## How-to Resource

- Detailed information can be found in the Interna-tional Existing Building Code, published by the International Code Council.

**Comparison of Cost:  Preventing vs. Repairing Earthquake Damage**

**Project Cost**          **Cost to Repair After an Earthquake**

Project and Repair costs can vary widely.

## The Problem

The large opening of a garage door and the weight of a second-story room built over the garage can result in the walls being too weak to withstand earthquake shaking.

When the narrow sections of the wall on each side of the opening are not reinforced or braced, the weakness is worse.

## How to Identify

✓ Is the garage door opening in line with the rest of the house? *(See Figure 26)*

  ➢ If this is the case, additional bracing **may not** be needed.

✓ Is the house shaped like *Figure 27*? If this is the case, are there braces or plywood panels around the garage door opening?

  ➢ If there are no braces or plywood panels, strengthening may be needed.

✓ Consult a licensed architect or engineer to determine the strengthening required.

## Remember

■ Many homes with this weakness have been severely damaged in past earthquakes.

*Office of Emergency Services*

**Figure 25** - This mountain home was built over a garage, and its walls were not strong enough to withstand an earthquake.

*HOUSE VIEWED FROM ABOVE*

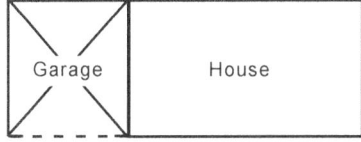

**Figure 26** - If the wall of the main house is in line with the wall containing the door of a garage with a room over it, the adjoining wall may help brace the garage.

*HOUSE VIEWED FROM ABOVE*

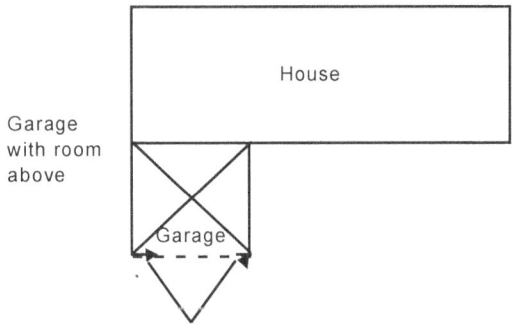

Wall may need bracing

**Figure 27 - Additional bracing.** Home configuration where there is no in-line wall. Additional bracing may be appropriate in this situation.

# Strengthen Rooms over Garages

## The Solution

Consult a licensed architect or engineer to design plywood paneling or a steel frame around the door opening *(See Figure 28)*.

Have plans drawn.

Obtain a permit from your local Building Department.

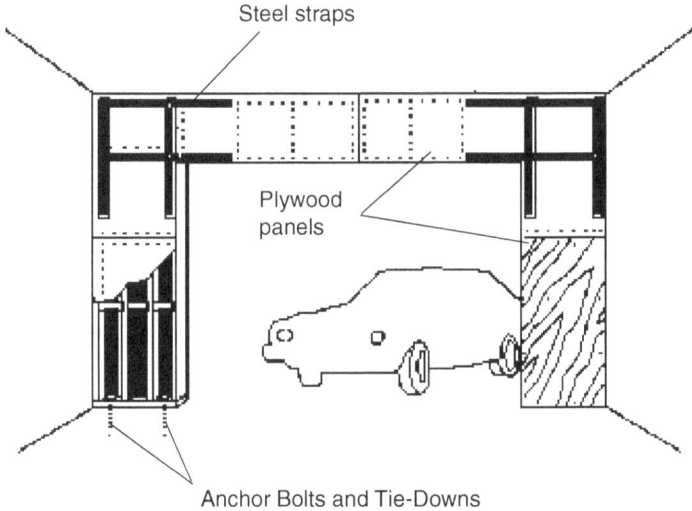

Steel straps

Plywood panels

Anchor Bolts and Tie-Downs

**Figure 28—Bracing garage walls.** If your house has a room over the garage, the garage walls may not be strong enough to hold up during an earthquake unless they are braced with plywood panels and steel straps.

## How-to Resource

■ Detailed information can be found in the <u>International Existing Building Code</u>, published by the International Code Council.

| Comparison of Cost:  Preventing vs. Repairing Earthquake Damage | |
| --- | --- |
| **Project Cost** | **Cost to Repair After an Earthquake** |
| $5,000 to $25,000 | $15,000 to total value of home (if completely destroyed) |

# OTHER EARTHQUAKE-RELATED CONCERNS

Unreinforced Masonry Chimneys

## The Problem

Many chimneys are built of unreinforced brick or stone. During an earthquake, these can collapse or break and fall on the roof.

When the chimney fails, the falling stones and bricks can:

- Cause injuries
- Damage the house
- Damage cars

Tall slender chimneys are most vulnerable.

*Office of Emergency Services*

**Figure 29** - This unreinforced chimney fell during a recent earthquake.

## How to Identify

✓ Check the mortar between the bricks or stones with a screwdriver. If it crumbles when you pick at it, the chimney may be a hazard.

✓ Inspect the attic and floor spaces for metal ties that should be holding the chimney to the house.

✓ Determining whether a chimney is susceptible to earthquake damage is not always easy. When in doubt, consult a licensed engineer or contractor.

## Remember

- Do not locate patios, children's play areas, or parking spaces near a questionable chimney.
- Tell family members to get away from chimneys and fireplaces during earthquakes.

*Guna Selvaduray*

**Figure 30 - Morgan Hill Earthquake.** Broken chimney fell on roof.

## The Solution

Tear down the old or damaged chimney and replace with a newly constructed chimney.

Several steps can be taken to reduce the risk of damage from falling chimneys, depending upon the type of chimney you have. They include:

- Add plywood panels at the roof or above the ceiling joists to prevent the brick or stone from falling into the house.

  * This can be done by layering plywood above the ceiling, in the house's attic, or nailing plywood under the shingles when reroofing.

- Replace the upper chimney with metal flues.

- Strengthen the existing chimney.

  * This can be a complicated process, depending upon the construction and height of the existing chimney.

Consult your local Building Department and obtain necessary permits first.

## How-to Resource

- Go to www.fema.gov, and under the Earthquake section, search for "Strengthen Chimneys" for specific strengthening instructions.

*California Seismic Safety Commission*

**Figure 31** - Photo showing damaged chimney removed. Note that the fireplace is now not functional.

| Comparison of Cost: Preventing vs. Repairing Earthquake Damage | |
| --- | --- |
| **Project Cost** | **Cost to Repair After an Earthquake** |
| $2,000 to $12,000 | $15,000 to total value of home (if completely destroyed) |

# Foundations

## No Foundation

**The Problem**  Some older houses were built on wood beams laid directly on the ground, without foundations. These houses may shift during earthquakes, causing structural damage and breaking utility lines.

**How to Identify**  Look under the house. If you see no concrete or masonry around the outside walls, the house may lack a foundation.

**What Can Be Done**  You may need to add a foundation to make the house earthquake resistant. Just as when strengthening or replacing an unreinforced masonry foundation, you will require the advice of a licensed architect, engineer, or foundation contractor.

## Old Concrete Foundation

**The Problem**  Some older concrete foundations were made with sand or stone that interacted chemically over time, and the concrete eventually crumbles and becomes too soft to withstand earthquake forces.

**How to Identify**  Inspect the foundation for large cracks in the concrete, concrete crumbling off the foundation, or concrete crumbling when you pick at it with a screwdriver.

**What Can Be Done**  You may need to replace some or all of the foundation. You should consult a licensed foundation contractor or an engineer.

# Homes with Unique Designs

**The Problem**

The design and construction features of some homes make them vulnerable to earthquake damage, especially if these homes are not specifically designed and built to resist earthquakes. Homes at risk are those with irregular shapes, large windows (which can break in earthquakes and scatter shards of glass), more than two stories, irregular walls, or porches and overhangs.

**How to Identify**

Many homes with these features are strong enough to withstand earthquakes and it is difficult to tell whether such homes need strengthening. If you have doubts about one or more of these features in your home, or in a home you are planning to buy, you should consult a licensed architect or engineer for an assessment.

**What Can Be Done**

A professional can advise you on how to identify and fix earthquake weaknesses if necessary. For example, large windows can be made safer by applying plastic film on them.

# NATURAL GAS SAFETY

## The Problem

Natural gas piping and appliances can be damaged during earthquakes, causing gas leaks.

If ignited, this can result in fires that can burn part of, or, the entire house.

About one in four fires after an earthquake is related to natural gas leaks.

Gas leaks after an earthquake are more likely if:

- There are structural weaknesses.
- Gas appliances are not anchored.
- Flexible pipe connections are not used.

The primary concern is property loss from fire damage.

The potential for life loss is limited since most single-family homes have several safe exits.

## How to Identify

✓ Examine all natural gas appliances (water heaters, dryers, stoves, ovens, furnaces) to see if they are anchored to the floor or walls, and have flexible pipe connections.

## Plan Ahead

Locate your gas meter outside your home.

Identify the exact location of the shutoff valve and make sure that you have access to it.

Make sure you have a wrench that is readily available to turn off the gas when needed.

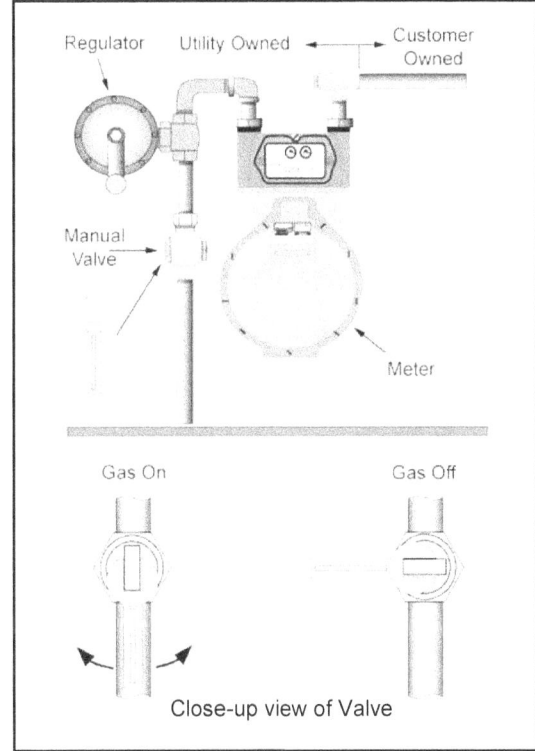

**Figure  32 - Manual shutoff valve location.**

## Manual Gas Shutoff

- The most cost-effective way to manage the risk from natural gas is to know how and when to manually shut off the gas.

- Use the wrench to turn off the manual valve located at the gas meter *(See Figure 32, page 25)*.

- Shut off your gas only if you:
  - Smell gas
  - Hear gas escaping
  - Suspect a broken gas pipe, appliance, vent, or flue

## Remember

- Once the gas has been shut off, service can be restored only by utility personnel or qualified plumbers.

- High demands for qualified personnel after an earthquake can lead to substantial delays in restoring natural gas service.

## Resources

- Go to www.fema.gov, and under the Earthquake section, search for "Retrofit Gas and Water Lines" for retrofitting instructions.

- Publication: Improving Natural Gas Safety in Earthquakes. California Seismic Safety Commission, Adopted July 11, 2002. Available online at http://www.seismic.ca.gov/pub/ CSSC_2002-03_Natural%20Gas%20Safety.pdf.

## Automatic Gas Shutoff Options

There are a variety of automatic gas shut-off valves available. These cost more than manual shutoff valves and may provide additional safety, but may also have some disadvantages.

The types of valves available include:

- Earthquake shake-actuated valves
- Excess flow valves
- Methane detectors
- Hybrid systems
- Others

These can be installed on the "customer owned" side of the gas meter.

Consult your local Building Department because:

- Some installations will require building permits.
- Some local jurisdictions have adopted ordinances requiring automatic gas shutoff devices at the time of sale or during significant renovations.

# GETTING THE WORK DONE

## PLANS, PERMITS, AND CONTRACTORS

- Decide which strengthening project or projects you are going to do.

- Get the necessary building permits first.

  - If you are "doing-it-yourself," you still need the proper permits.

  - For more complex projects, have a licensed architect or engineer draw up the necessary plans and specifications.

    - ✓ Interview two or three architects or engineers.

    - ✓ Ask for references or former clients.

    - ✓ Talk to references or former clients.

    - ✓ Compare experience, ideas, and fees.

  - Submit the plans for approval to your local building department.

  - Remember: the building codes are designed for your safety.

There are many publications that describe strengthening projects in detail.

Visit the California Seismic Safety Commission's website at www.seismic.ca.gov, which provides many useful links.

- Get the documents that relate to your project and read them.

  - This will help you to better understand what the architect or engineer is doing, and also what the contractor is doing.

- The International Existing Building Code Appendix Chapter 3 contains the best current guidelines. Ask your local Building Department to review a copy.

- Select your licensed contractor.

  - First make sure the contractor is properly licensed.

  - Interview at least two or three contractors.

  - Ask your licensed architect or engineer for recommendations.

  - Ask for references or former clients.

  - Talk to references or former clients.

  - Compare experience, fees, and terms of contract.

  - Get at least three written bids for the construction work.

  - The lowest bid may not be the best bid.

- Keep all plans, permits, and other records of your strengthening project.

  - Provide future buyers of your home with these.

If your home has been designated as "historical," you also may need to comply with local regulations regarding historical structures.

- Contact your local Building Department for further help with this.

### REMEMBER

Whether you do it yourself, or hire a contractor, **you need permits** from your local Building Department.

It costs far less to correct earthquake weaknesses before an earthquake than to repair the damage after an earthquake.

If your home is damaged in an earthquake, you will probably also have other costs such as lodging, medical, etc.

## DON'T HESITATE - MITIGATE!

# AFTER A DISASTER –

## *HIRE A LICENSED CONTRACTOR!*

### After a Disaster...

**DO NOT:**

- Rush into repairs, no matter how badly they are needed.

- Hire the first contractor who comes along.

- Accept verbal promises.

**DO:**

- Get proof that the person you are dealing with is a licensed contractor appropriate for the work to be done.

- Get the contractor's license number and verify that it is current and valid.

- Get a written contract that contains all the details of the job to be performed.

- Get at least three bids.

- Check references of other work the contractor has done, if possible, in your area.

- Develop a payment schedule with the contractor.

- Consider a completion bond on large projects.

### Avoid Payment Pitfalls

- Try to limit your down payment. Some State laws limit the amount of money a contractor can request as a down payment. Contact your State or local consumer agency to find out what the law is in your area.

- Try to make payments during the project contingent on completion of a defined amount of work. This way, if the work is not proceeding according to schedule, the payments are also delayed.

- Withhold at least 10% of the total contract price until the project is complete.

- Do not make final payment until:
  - The building department has signed off on it,
  - You are satisfied with the job, and
  - You take a final walk-through to make sure work is complete and done correctly.

# GEOLOGIC HAZARDS

Sellers of real estate may be required to disclose to buyers certain information regarding natural hazards that can affect the property being sold. In addition to flood and fire hazard information, disclosure of seismic hazards may also be required.

This section:

- Describes briefly the basic geology-related hazards, and

- Introduces the government mapping programs that define which areas are susceptible to those hazards.

### Ground Shaking:

- Ground shaking causes 99% of the earthquake damage to homes.

- Areas near large active faults are more likely to be shaken severely than areas in the rest of the state.

### Landslide:

- Earthquakes can also trigger landslides.

- Earthquake shaking can cause the soil and rock to slide off a slope, ripping apart homes on the slope and/or crushing homes downhill *(See Figure 33).*

### Fault Rupture:

- An actual crack forms and the ground is offset along the two sides of a fault during an earthquake *(See Figure 34).*

- A house built over an active fault can be torn apart if the ground ruptures beneath it.

- If the house is built over a "creeping" fault – one that moves slowly with no earthquakes or a series of very small earthquakes – the damage may not be noticed for some time.

Patrica Grossi and Augustin Rodriguez, EERI

**Figure 33 - Landslide, San Simeon Earthquake, December 22, 2003.** Landslides on San Gregorio Road in Atascadero, California, only a short distance away from where the homes with the most damage were located.

Robert A. Eplett, OES, CA

**Figure 34 - Fault Rupture.** Landers Earthquake of June 28, 1992, produced a surface rupture of over 50 miles along faults in the Mojave Desert.

### Lateral Spreading:

- Intense shaking during an earthquake can cause the soil to break into blocks that move apart from each other. This can cause damage to the foundation of a house *(See Figure 35).*

### Liquefaction:

- During earthquakes, loose, wet sandy soil can become almost like quicksand, and lose its ability to support structures. This can cause the foundation of a house to sink, break, or tilt *(See Figure 36).*

### Tsunami:

- A tsunami is a series of large sea waves caused by an underwater earthquake or landslide.

- Coastal areas are prone to tsunami damage.

- Tsunami waves can come from a great distance and can cause flooding or wash away houses in low-lying areas along the shore.

### Dam Failure:

- Earthquake damage to a dam can cause sudden and devastating flooding of houses downstream.

- During the 1971 San Fernando Earthquake, the Lower San Fernando Dam above the San Fernando Valley was damaged. Had it failed, it would have flooded the homes below, causing many deaths and injuries. *(See Figure 37).* Risk of an aftershock forced residents in an 11-square-mile area to evacuate for the next 3 days.

### Recommendation:

If you live in a low-lying coastal area or a dam inundation zone, become familiar with evacuation routes to higher ground and be prepared to evacuate such areas immediately after an earthquake.

**Figure 35 - Lateral Spreading, Loma Prieta Earthquake, October 17, 1989.** Lateral spreading damaged levee road along the San Lorenzo River.

**Figure 36 - Loma Prieta Earthquake, October 17, 1989.** Lateral spreading, liquefaction and sand boils caused extensive damage in the Marina District of San Francisco, about 60 miles away from the epicenter.

**Figure 37 -** Lower San Fernando Dam that was badly damaged by the 1971 San Fernando Earthquake.

# Earthquake Hazard Mapping

Enormous progress has been made in understanding how, why, and where earthquakes occur. This has led to the creation of maps that highlight areas having the highest likelihood of damaging earthquakes.

Five mapping programs have been developed to help people lead safer lives in earthquake country.

## U.S. Geologic Survey National Seismic Hazard Maps

The USGS provides seismic hazard assessments for the United States and areas around the world. These hazard maps serve as the basis for seismic provisions used in building codes and influence billions of dollars of new construction every year. For more information about seismic hazard analysis, the USGS maps, and the underlying data on which they are based, visit the USGS website at http://earthquake.usgs.gov/hazmaps/.

The earthquake hazards map on page 3 of this Guide is based on the USGS Seismic Hazard Map for the Coterminous United States, available from the USGS website at http://eqhazmaps.usgs.gov/html/map_graphic.html.

## Earthquake Fault Zone Maps

These maps show active earthquake faults prone to surface ruptures and identify a 1,000-foot-wide zone with the fault line at the center.

## Seismic Hazard Zone Maps

These maps show areas where landslides and liquefaction are most likely to occur during earthquakes.

## Tsunami Inundation and Evacuation Route Maps

Maps for the Pacific Coast show areas where low-lying regions are exposed to tsunami inundation. These maps are in various stages of preparation and availability. More information about tsunamis and tsunami mapping is available from the National Tsunami Hazard Mitigation Program, Center for Tsunami Inundation Mapping Efforts, at http://www.pmel.noaa.gov/tsunami/time/.

## Dam Inundation Maps

These maps show the areas below major dams that may be flooded in the event of their failure.

## How Are These Maps Used?

The zones defined by the maps are at greatest potential risk when a major earthquake occurs. This is particularly the case when the earthquake occurs during or shortly after a heavy rainfall, which increases the likelihood of liquefaction and landslides.

Special geotechnical studies are required before buildings can be built in Earthquake Fault Zones or Seismic Hazard Zones.

Your local building or planning department can show you copies of USGS seismic hazard maps and other earthquake hazard maps that may be available for your community.

*The seller of real estate within a hazard zone may be required to disclose that the property lies within such a zone at the time of sale.*

# WHAT TO DO *DURING* AN EARTHQUAKE

## DROP!

## COVER!

## HOLD ON!

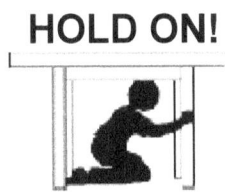

1. IF YOU ARE **INDOORS**—STAY THERE! "**DROP, COVER, AND HOLD ON.**" Get under a sturdy desk or table and hang on to it, or move into a hallway or get against an inside wall. Stay clear of windows, fireplaces, and heavy furniture or appliances. Get out of the kitchen, which is a dangerous place in earthquakes since it's full of things that can fall on you. Don't run downstairs or rush outside while the building is shaking or while there is danger of falling and hurting yourself or being hit by falling glass or debris.

2. IF YOU ARE **OUTSIDE**—**GET INTO THE OPEN**, away from buildings, power lines, chimneys, and anything else that might fall on you.

3. IF YOU ARE **DRIVING**—**STOP**, but carefully. Move your car as far out of traffic as possible. Do not stop on or under a bridge or overpass or under trees, light posts, power lines, or signs. Stay inside your car until the shaking stops. When you resume driving, watch for breaks in the pavement, fallen rocks, and bumps in the road.

4. IF YOU ARE ON OR NEAR A **STEEP HILLSIDE, WATCH OUT FOR LANDSLIDES**, falling rock, trees, and other debris that could be loosened by earthquakes.

## If You Feel a Strong Earthquake or Receive a Tsunami Warning When You are on the Coast

1. **DROP, COVER, AND HOLD ON.** Watch for falling objects until the earthquake is over.

2. **MOVE TO HIGHER GROUND** or inland away from the coast immediately. A tsunami may be coming. Go on foot if possible. The first waves may reach the coast within minutes after the ground shaking stops. The first wave is almost never the largest. Later waves may be spaced tens of minutes apart and can continue arriving for many hours.

3. **THERE MAY BE NO TIME FOR AUTHORITIES TO ISSUE A WARNING.** If you do not hear an evacuation announcement, but notice a sudden drop or rise in water level or hear a loud noise coming from the water, nature may be warning you of impending danger.

4. **STAY AWAY FROM THE COAST.** Do not return to the shore after the first wave. Waves may continue to arrive for hours.

5. **LISTEN TO A RADIO FOR AN "ALL CLEAR"** before returning to the shore.

# WHAT TO DO *BEFORE* AN EARTHQUAKE

*The information contained in this section does not represent weaknesses in the earthquake resistance of homes. It is valuable information to keep in mind to reduce risks to yourself, your family, and your home. These lists are only highlights of the actions you should take.*

## Gather Emergency Supplies

*Be sure you have these basic supplies on hand:*

- ❑ Fire extinguisher
- ❑ Adequate supplies of medications that you or family members are taking
- ❑ Crescent and pipe wrenches to turn off gas and water supplies
- ❑ First-aid kit and handbook
- ❑ Flashlights with extra bulbs and fresh batteries
- ❑ Portable battery-powered radio or television and extra fresh batteries
- ❑ Water for each family member for at least 3 days (allow at least 1 gallon per person per day) and purification tablets or chlorine bleach to purify drinking water from other sources
- ❑ Canned and packaged foods, enough for 3 days, and at least an additional 4-day supply readily accessible for use if you are confined to home. Don't forget a mechanical can opener and extra pet food!
- ❑ Camp stove or barbecue to cook on outdoors (store fuel out of the reach of children)
- ❑ Waterproof, heavy-duty plastic bags for waste disposal
- ❑ Copies of personal identification, such as driver's licenses, passports, and work identification badges, and copies of medical prescriptions and credit cards
- ❑ An extra set of car keys and house keys
- ❑ Matches in waterproof container
- ❑ Map of the area marked with places you could go and their telephone numbers
- ❑ Cash and coins
- ❑ Special items, such as denture needs, contact lenses and supplies, extra eyeglasses, and hearing aid batteries
- ❑ Items for seniors, disabled persons, or anyone with serious allergies
- ❑ Items for infants, such as formula, diapers, bottles, pacifiers, powdered milk, and medications not requiring refrigeration

## Plan Ahead

1. Create a family disaster plan; practice and maintain the plan.
2. Make and complete a checklist.
3. Plan home escape routes.
4. Conduct fire and emergency evacuation drills at least twice a year and include your pets in your evacuation and sheltering drills.
5. Test your smoke alarms once a month (daylight savings time or birthdays) and replace batteries at least once a year in battery-powered smoke alarms.
6. Make sure each member of your family knows what to do no matter where they are when earthquakes occur.

   - Establish two meeting places where you can all reunite afterward: one right outside your home, in case of a sudden emergency, and one outside your neighborhood in case you cannot return home or are asked to leave your neighborhood.
   - Find out about the earthquake plan developed by your children's school or day care.
   - Remember that since transportation may be disrupted, you may have to stay at your workplace for a day or two following a major earthquake. Keep some emergency supplies—food, liquids, and comfortable shoes, for example—at work.
   - Pick two out-of-town contacts:
     - A friend or relative who will be your household's **primary** contact,
     - A friend or relative who will be your household's **alternative** contact.

7. Know where your gas, electric, and water main shutoffs are and how to turn them off if there is a leak or electrical short; if in doubt, ask your utility companies. Make sure that all the older members of your family can shut off the utilities.
8. Locate your nearest fire and police stations and emergency medical facility. Remember that telephones may not work after an earthquake. If you can, use your land line rather than your cell phone to call 911, but only if you need emergency help.
9. Talk to your neighbors—how could they help you, or you help them, after an earthquake?
10. Take a Red Cross first aid and cardiopulmonary resuscitation (CPR) training course.
11. Make arrangements with friends or relatives to temporarily house **your pets** after disasters because emergency shelters will not accept pets.
12. If your home is located near a steep hillside, in an area near the shore of a body of water or below a dam, check with your local building or planning department to see if you are in a landslide, tsunami or dam inundation zone. Plan for how, when, and where your family should evacuate.

# WHAT TO DO *AFTER* AN EARTHQUAKE

*Wear sturdy shoes to avoid injury from broken glass and debris.*
*Expect aftershocks.*

## Check for Injuries

1. If a person is bleeding, put direct pressure on the wound. Use clean gauze or cloth, if available.
2. If a person is not breathing, administer rescue breathing. The front pages of many telephone books contain instructions on how to do it along with detailed instructions on other first-aid measures.
3. Do not attempt to move seriously injured persons unless they are in immediate danger of further injury.
4. Cover injured persons with blankets to keep them warm.
5. Seek medical help for serious injuries.

## Check for Hazards

1. *Fire or fire hazards.* Put out fires in your home or neighborhood immediately. Call for help, but don't wait for the fire department.
2. *Gas leaks.* Shut off the main gas valve only if you suspect a leak because of broken pipes or the odor of natural gas. Don't turn it back on yourself—wait for the gas company to check for leaks.
3. *Damaged electrical wiring.* Shut off power at the control box if there is any damage to your house wiring.
4. *Downed or damaged utility lines.* Do not touch downed power lines or any objects in contact with them.
5. *Spills.* Clean up any spilled medicines, drugs, or other potentially harmful materials such as bleach, lye, and gasoline or other hazardous materials.
6. *Downed or damaged chimneys.* Approach chimneys with caution. They may be weakened and could topple during aftershocks. Don't use a fireplace with a damaged chimney—it could start a fire or let poisonous gases into your house.
7. *Fallen items.* Beware of items tumbling off shelves when you open the doors of closets and cupboards.

## Check Your Food and Water Supplies

1. If power is off, plan meals to use up foods that will spoil quickly, or frozen foods. If you keep the door closed, food in your freezer should be good for at least a couple of days.

2. Don't light your kitchen stove if you suspect a gas leak.

3. Use barbecues or camp stoves, outdoors only, for emergency cooking.

4. If your water is off, you can drink supplies from water heaters, melted ice cubes, or canned vegetables. Try to avoid drinking water from swimming pools or, especially, spas—it may have too many chemicals in it to be safe.

## Do Not . . .

- **Do not** eat or drink anything from open containers near shattered glass.

- **Do not** turn the gas on again if you turned it off; let the gas company do it.

- **Do not** use matches, lighters, camp stoves or barbecues, electrical equipment—including telephones—or appliances until you are sure there are no gas leaks. They may create sparks that could ignite leaking gas and cause an explosion and fire.

- **Do not** use your telephone, except for a medical or fire emergency. You could tie up lines needed for emergency response.
  If you need help and the phone doesn't work, send someone for help.

- **Do not** expect firefighters, police, or paramedics to help you right away. They may not be available.

# RESOURCE ORGANIZATIONS

*Some of the organizations listed below have information to help you strengthen your home against earthquakes and help you and your family prepare a personal earthquake response plan. Other resources that can help you may be available in your community; check your local telephone directory.*

## Structural Safety Information

### American Institute of Architects
Local chapters have referral lists of licensed architects; consult telephone directory listing for "American Institute of Architects."
http://www.aia.org

### American Society of Civil Engineers
1801 Alexander Bell Drive
Reston, VA 20191
Telephone: (800) 548-2723
http://www.asce.org

### American Society of Home Inspectors
932 Lee Street, Suite 101
Des Plaines, IL 60016
Telephone: (800) 743-2744
http://www.ashi.com
Referral list of licensed inspectors.

### Federal Emergency Management Agency
Headquarters
500 C Street, SW.
Washington, DC 20472
Telephone: (800) 621-FEMA
http://www.fema.gov

FEMA provides a wide variety of information suitable for the homeowner, including the availability of, and registration for, Federal disaster aid programs after a damaging earthquake or other disasters.

### International Code Council
5203 Leesburg Pike, Suite 600
Falls Church, VA 22041
Telephone: 1-888-ICC-SAFE
http://www.iccsafe.org

### National Council of Structural Engineers Associations
645 N. Michigan Avenue, Suite 540
Chigago, IL 60611
Telephone: (312) 649-4600
http://www.ncsea.com

### National Fire Protection Association
1 Batterymarch Park
Quincy, MA 02169
Telephone: (617) 770-3000
http://www.nfpa.org

## Geologic Information

### United States Geological Survey
National Center
12201 Sunrise Valley Drive
Reston, VA 20192
Telephone: 1-888-ASK-USGS
http://earthquake.usgs.gov

This is the Federal agency responsible for geological and earthquake hazard research, mapping, and policy. It provides maps and other information to the general public.

### States, Cities, and Counties
Consult your telephone directory under State, city, or county government listings for the office of emergency services or disaster management; city or county building and planning department; and State, city, or county government geologist.

## Emergency Planning Information

### American Red Cross
Consult your telephone directory for the address and phone number of your local chapter.
http://www.redcross.org

**Federal Emergency Management Agency**

Headquarters
500 C Street, SW.
Washington, DC 20472
Telephone: (800) 621-FEMA
http://www.fema.gov

www.ingramcontent.com/pod-product-compliance
Lightning Source LLC
Chambersburg PA
HW080629290526
CB00007B/2984